fault
tree

other works by kathryn l. pringle

RIGHT NEW BIOLOGY, Factory School, 2009

CHAPBOOKS

The Stills, Duration Press
Temper and Felicity are lovers, TAXT

fault tree

kathryn l. pringle

OMNIDAWN PUBLISHING

RICHMOND, CALIFORNIA

2012

Cover art: "flipclock"
by Chris Vitiello

Book cover and interior design by Cassandra Smith

green press
INITIATIVE

Omnidawn Publishing is committed to preserving ancient
forests and natural resources. We elected to print this title on
30% postconsumer recycled paper, processed chlorine-free. As
a result, for this printing, we have saved:

2 Trees (40' tall and 6-8" diameter)
860 Gallons of Wastewater
1 million BTUs of Total Energy
54 Pounds of Solid Waste
191 Pounds of Greenhouse Gases

Omnidawn Publishing made this paper choice because our
printer, Thomson-Shore, Inc., is a member of Green Press
Initiative, a nonprofit program dedicated to supporting authors,
publishers, and suppliers in their efforts to reduce their use of
fiber obtained from endangered forests.

For more information, visit www.greenpressinitiative.org

Environmental impact estimates were made using the Environmental Defense
Paper Calculator. For more information visit: www.edf.org/papercalculator

Library of Congress Cataloging-in-Publication Data

Pringle, Kathryn L.
  Fault tree / Kathryn L. Pringle.
    p. cm.
  ISBN 978-1-890650-70-4 (trade pbk. : alk. paper)
  I. Title.
  PS3616.R548F38 2012
  811'.6--dc23
                        2012014449

Published by Omnidawn Publishing, Richmond, California
www.omnidawn.com   (510) 237-5472   (800) 792-4957
        10 9 8 7 6 5 4 3 2 1
        ISBN: 978-1-890650-70-4

Acknowledgments:

Thanks to the editors of the following journals for publishing portions of *fault tree: bang out sf, Fence, Past Simple, Raleigh Quarterly, Try,* and the anthology *Conversations at the Wartime Café: A Decade of War 2001 -2011.*

My deep appreciation goes to Erika Staiti, Kate Schapira, Elise Ficarra, Chris Vitiello, Kate Greenstreet, Guillermo Parra, Dianne Timblin, and Carrie Hunter for their careful attention to this manuscript. Without you, this book could not have happened. Thank you!

Thanks also to Jamie Lewis, Ken Rumble, Tanya Olson, Amy White, Molly Renda, Joseph Donahue, Des Peterson, Cynthia Sailers, Samantha Giles, Judith Goldman, David Buuck, Stephanie Young, CA Conrad, Michael Nicoloff, Jessica Smith, Stacy Doris, Gillian Conoley, Maxine Chernoff, D.A. Powell, Myung Mi Kim, Toni Mirosevich, Charles Hood, and Terry Ehret for art, inspiration, exercise, and argument.

I am especially grateful to C.D. Wright and the folks at Omnidawn for helping *fault tree* come into the world.

for my teacher, Stacy Doris
and my father, Greg Pringle

Fault tree analysis (FTA) *is a failure analysis in which an undesired state of a system is analyzed using Boolean logic to combine a series of lower-level events. This analysis method is mainly used in the field of safety engineering to quantitatively determine the probability of a safety hazard.*
http://en.wikipedia.org/wiki/Fault_tree_analysis

It might appear possible to overcome all the difficulties attending the definition of "time" by substituting "the position of the small hand of my watch" for "time." And in fact such a definition is satisfactory when we are concerned with defining time exclusively for the place where the watch is located; but it is no longer satisfactory when we have to connect in time a series of events occurring at different places, or – what comes to the same thing – to evaluate the times of events occurring at places remote from the watch.

Albert Einstein, *On the Electrodynamics of Moving Bodies*

once the moment came it was too late to go back to the moments before it. that's the problem with time. we can't control it.

it had been my desire to remain in the pre-moment state but time disallowed this. vehemently. i took precautions. i invested in the pre-moment. i built a future in the moment that came before the moment that undid the future that was never to be a moment. and now i walk away from the nonmoment directly toward foreseeable moments. it is the commonness that kills me. each moment. it has been hard living since the pre-moment. daily reminders of the same things. the daily wait.

there isn't much here that i don't know—that i'm not accustomed to. sometimes i wonder if maybe i'm supposed to be learning to appreciate the beating that the daily habits of others inflicts upon me. perhaps i was too pleased with myself. before the moment.

the moment was like falling asleep. sometimes i think i am asleep. but for the sleep's duration...

book1/WANT is a stationary CLOCK/ involutions

Every particular actual thing lays upon the universe the obligation of conforming to it.... We conform to our bodily organs and to the vague world which lies beyond them.

A.N. Whitehead, Symbolism, Its Meaning and Effect

in order to get off the island you first have to build an airstrip that is long enough for the biplane to build up enough speed to take off.

the island is not at any point long or wide enough to build an airstrip for the biplane to take off.

therefore you are not leaving this island.

the show was canceled because we were all killed last night

we are to be at the studio by 8:30 am and you are still in boxer shorts.

the car is coming to pick us up to take us to the studio.

i know you are embezzling money into a private account:
26 million dollars.

last night i was shot through the head
three times clean through
and then the heart
but the sponsors have made a huge stink and we are to be at the studio
in approximately 33 minutes – and you are in yr boxers – you must be
conniving with those legs of yours

this is the PAST we are in the PAST and in the PAST i am alive

they slit my throat, too.

in order to get off the island you first have to build an airstrip : i don't know why you landed here in the first place : we could all see from the sky that there would not be enough room to leave: i feel the pull of water how many planes will fall : how many : times will you land us here :

what is shocking is that the ferry only appears as near as you believe you
can swim

they put the disease in the ice cream and ship it out that way

the disease must be frozen
the ferry comes within one mile of the distance you can swim–fully
rested

sometimes a lamp tells you where more than just the cracks are
in the ceiling

THERE THROUGH TIME

the flat world is hard for the facing
i walk into things before i know i'm there
i see what i think i see
engagement takes practice

my hand, outstretched, reaches to touch yr hand, also outstretched, but no
touch
only air

a person can be a dot
a dot against a background
might as well be the background

and you are gone, now

a wall, a painting, a kitchen counter

my blind spot

of course, one could make the argument that you were never there
which is problematic
for me being situated more or less
outside of you who
may or may not be
there or anywhere

if you exist in the future
then i am chasing you
or just behind

for example, if the placement of clocks takes place
prior to the synchronization of clocks
then time cannot be in agreement

however, if clock A is synchronized to clock B
and clock C is synchronized to clock A
and then, post-synchronization, all clocks are placed

only then will i know if i am chasing you
or you are chasing me

could you maybe shimmer
so i can hold a place?

or am i now just mere
am i now of nothing
or not much of anything
or am i now a speck
of something that was?

THERE THROUGH SPACE

for the sake of language   we are not keeping time
(a foundation built counter)

the binding of what is perceived is
bent, actually is bent, but you won't see it
hanging there

drawn

outside sounds like rain
but is rocks

pebbles hitting bowls of water

we (through definitions) stall.
stall. is mental
poise. two reeds bedded down

the open out of
stutter
all lay low
keep still
stand –
closed eyes

then as now we cannot see so cannot be seen

we occur in simultaneity
the aged, the ease

(the first to go is the time)

SUSPECT time

a most specific stall

time comprehension goes unseen

it does
not happen
it has

today it is never 9:30

∴ we sleep when tired

i'm not saying this to scare you but goodbye.

first goodbye.
and then
examine attachment (in seconds, s)
akin to

<u>attachment</u>
seconds

if recognition is destroyed, what then of attachment?

whether my body is rigid, stippled, perpendicular
or not, i am a floater

the precision of my rigid body in motion
has been mathematically proven
to be equal to the accuracy of my body at rest

in this place, that is

at this time

that is

or is
not

you will see it as
my own tenacious grip
on a silver cord

first, though

the snow fell up to thirty inches, melted ten, and then we had ice

my transistor was hemorrhaging

exposed wires bleeding

giving off heat

in the form of steam

i'm inclined to say that the wires were bleeding yellow and green ooze but it was really blood like any other kind of blood. which is to say it was red. RED.

even better, and this is true, i was opened up and spewing (the transistor) on the frozen sidewalk in front of the hospital.

this was yesterday.

yesterday i was alive.

today always happens and so it feels like it never really happens because i am so well-versed in today and how it goes

you wake up or you *wake up*

most people wake up

i met a woman who said she had faith

in people waking up *waking up*

in people actually being

woken up

"with the TRUTH"

as an open-handed counterblow

to what is

we didn't get on well

but by the time i knew it

i was laden with her

i think it is better and kinder to wake slowly

instills a sense of achievement

in the waker

but she thought that was manipulation

that was the end of a continuously unhappening relationship

if time goes how it goes

we are still talking

and still in relation

regret is absolute confession

painted on the faces of each vessel

only minds wear a disguise

bodies revolt

one being exterior

naturally judges interiors

you have to be careful who you tell

because you tell and tell

you never stop telling

you tell someone suspect, someone

yr not sure you want to tell

you become infinitely

(you will infinitely tell, there's no escape from the infinite)

responsible not only for the telling but for the translation

of that situation's speechmaking

i'm a verb and you are a modifier

the difference between us is i only have one color

i say this knowing you, being prone to averages, will only half agree

as if you can really see me

it is in moments like this that language is just noise

which is to say that language is noise

what happens is you make me

and we either get along

because i like what you made

with what i got or we don't

because yr not much of an artist

this is how it goes with me and i say this with love

before i was killed i had to take one pill to stay alive and several pills to handle the side effects caused by the one pill that was keeping me alive:

Citalopram hydrobromide (aka Celexa®)[1]: 20 mg per day. a psychoanaleptic. disorder : anxiety.[2]

Orlistat (aka XENICAL®)[3] (aka Alli™)[4]. 3 times per day. dietary fat inhibitor. disorder: obesity.[5]

Glipzide (aka Glucotrol®XL).[6] 5 mg per day. glycemic control. disorder: type 2 diabetes mellitus.[7]

Phenobarbital (aka Phenobarbital).[8] 120 mg per day. seizures. disorder: seizures.[9]

---

[1] Citalopram's mechanism of action is presumably linked to potentiation of serotonergic activity in the central nervous system as a result from its inhibition of neuronal reuptake of serotonin. Animal studies have suggested that citalopram is a highly selective serotonin reuptake inhibitor (SSRI) having minimal effects on norepinephrine (NE) and dopamine (DA) neuronal reuptake. Tolerance to the inhibition of serotonin uptake is not induced by long-term treatment of rats with Celexa®. Citalopram is a racemic mixture (50/50). http://www.anxiety-and-depression-solutions.com/articles/conventional/pharmaceutical/celexa.php

[2] it became apparent that one of me was entertaining the thought of suicide and attempting to achieve this end by constantly playing scenes of our own tragic death (by hanging, by fire, decapitation by train, starvation, shot to the head, three shots to the heart just to say we love you frank stanford). these detailed scenes began to haunt the other of me and that me, who wanted to live, came to the conclusion that in order to live, one would have to die.

[3] XENICAL® (orlistat) is a lipase inhibitor for obesity management that acts by inhibiting the absorption of dietary fats. XENICAL is indicated for obesity management including weight loss and weight maintenance when used in conjunction with a reduced-calorie diet. XENICAL® is also indicated to reduce the risk for weight regain after prior weight loss. XENICAL® is indicated for obese patients with an initial body mass index (BMI) ≥ 30 kg/m^2 or ≥ 27 kg/m^2 in the presence of other risk factors (eg, hypertension, diabetes, dyslipidemia). Based on fecal fat measurements, the effect of XENICAL® is seen as soon as 24 to 48 hours after dosing. Upon discontinuation of therapy, fecal fat content usually returns to pretreatment levels within 48 to 72 hours. http://www.rxlist.com/xenical-drug.htm

[4] alli is different than Xenical® because it offers informational materials with the actual product. The alli starter pack includes over 200 pages of free in-pack materials to help guide individuals through the alli program and set expectations for gradual weight loss, help them make healthy eating choices, monitor daily diets, and manage treatment effects. Eighty percent of patients found these materials to be very helpful. Overall, the alli program offers unprecedented support and resources designed to help modify behavior by creating self-assessment and self-management skills. Assuming personal responsibility is integral to achieving sustainable weight loss. http://www.rxlist.com/alli-drug.htm

[5] despite my daily caloric burn of 2,000 cals and intake of 1,500 cals

[6] Glipizide is used to treat type 2 diabetes (condition in which the body does not use insulin normally and therefore cannot control the amount of sugar in the blood), particularly in people whose diabetes cannot be controlled by diet alone. Glipizide lowers blood sugar by stimulating the pancreas to secrete insulin and helping the body use insulin efficiently. The pancreas must be capable of producing insulin for this medication to work. Glipizide is not used to treat type 1 diabetes (condition in which the body does not produce insulin and therefore cannot control the amount of sugar in the blood). http://www.ncbi.nlm.nih.gov/pubmedhealth/PMH0000834

[7] See Obesity.

[8] Phenobarbital, a barbiturate, is used to control epilepsy (seizures) and as a sedative to relieve anxiety. It is also used for short-term treatment of insomnia to help you fall asleep.

but then i was killed.

book2/ THE END WORKED THE IDENTITY

she is going to write a book and first we will all be embarrassed of this
book and then you will all be proud of this book she has written and i
will be alone. she is going to write a book that embarrasses the family
and everyone will read it and wonder why i was wrong but i'm not wrong
it is embarrassing and the world will know that i am dead even though
i am on this couch in the dark grappling with the digital – clutching my
electric razor (most assuredly charged) daring it to show 9 o'clock once
again and never 9 thirty. mark me.

… the evolution of the art of war, which was collectively discussed and carefully structured and revised before writing commenced…

The Second World War: Asia and the Pacific
By John H. Bradley, Thomas Griess, Jack W. Dice

i did not like the version of myself that was raised firmly middle-class

it did not serve me

so i grew up poor white trash.

this explains everything and i could end here.

(you don't like the end.)

you must be complacent, you aged
ones, or we shall medicate you

shall
stall
stall

all burdens matter to trains

the tree faults
hold all expected digressions

prognosis is suspiciously as we make it

whether the physician (s)

can convince me to it

the family is first.
the family does the bidding
of most physicians

invisibly, revoking i

    the family as a substantial
    unit exercises this communal
    decree

HERE WRITES OUR HOUSE
WITHOUT THE OPEN

the air which is less

you aged
in darkness darkening

° to which
a counterpart
is more a distraction –
the identic response

take care.

the patient resembles a case i am misremembering

hospitals remind doctors you are human because it is good for business

a war

four entries for incidental
under my thumb–
one is for estuary
as well as
escapism

my free eye is landing on monopoly
pig-penned in dirty brackets
a tagline reads:

envelope her

while my line fails to translate this into something more
or that it should be more

we haven't always asked the questions we know the answers
we know the rates of evaporation
we know the tacky pages

my friend, tell me about the war

which one

all is war
we haven't not had one

i want to know about the war in yr time
what you did

what did you do thirty years before me

i don't know what was done

i know the bombs fell on all countries

i know that children were killed

i know that i can't hide on either side

there are four entries for incidental
under my thumb –

one is for rancor
as well as
insistence

the mattress became hard after two years and so they had to buy
another mattress
and maybe in two years it will become hard
but aren't they
supposed to soften
with time
the mattresses

aren't they

edges that are undefined

infinite

capable

i would say to describe her

how she opens her eyes

in the morning

and then smiles

but we were discussing the war
or asking questions about it

an interrogator

an interrogated

i did not, in fact, do anything

but vote against the war

by voting against the man who would vote for the war

and then i got sent to war
and i was thinking of this
while writing this
and of my children
who may ask

if i have children

if the mattress softens

aha
we must soften
the mattress

it will save us money

in the future

crosswalking in japan
or following a curve

is really incidental

or really not so different

when manufacturing yr independence
and the beauty of it
this moment

when the light

the light

the light

takes itself in care
to another

describe it in this way
not tragic
only true.

crosswalk

o, yes. the crosswalk

had been slicked
because of rain

or the rain slicked
the crosswalk

however you sense it

by light

the light and the beauty of the light
not want

descry
in this way
or conceive.

as in to take into

the mouth whole

the lips extend

the teeth held

back not to

puncture the object

tongue relaxed

depressed in such

a way as to

make way

for object object

who has temporary dominion

an over-subtle register in opposition to a vote of confidence
[the swing has swung, so to speak]

you taped the to-be-executed eyes
back of the head clasped
laid it down on the floor beside his feet

he was about to be conducted
is what he was

except the pacing was all wrong for death
we know it will not come until it comes
so, he waited

as some people do, ones of us more actively
than others of us but all to the same end
we are betrothed

that train line was never meant to go through town
the politicians had said one thing while padding another thing
as we all know

we waited on a politician's survival mechanism to engage
but so few are real animals
that it was not a big surprise when it didn't

and tracks were laid
and trains were running
and the town was divided

people who were family
people who were friends
people who were haters of each other

each had to resolve themselves with a different center

a place divided in half

now twin-tracked nuclei

what is observed is not always what is perceived

HERE

we are conductor
as force moves a sum
HERE depends

we imagine
precise equal rest
together

the means moving bodies
relatively, the earth
infilled in as much as union rests
emanations render
unmuted
an inkling,

s o i s e a l w e l l s

but they spring

this moment has false permanence

i fail in this moment
however

GIVEN
that moment is resistance
encircled,
never an   utterance

betweenness an elemental

we two color echo sleeps sounds out between lips breathe

midrib, where a poison

of muscle and veins

stand

OF/F

      yielding
               PERCUSSIVE

          attunement

          an instance of
          remembering

shaped in a circle soft chalk serial numbers beneath
the upturned dumpster's neckline
resembling graffiti

wheeled, wield

to walk through a field and feel wind and feel sun is what some of us
consider a well-lived living

how it goes not now

is that fiscal effort

is more becoming a man in a suit

unencumbered, unenlisted

i had more than half my teeth.
was over five feet tall
and literate

i waited until i had graduated from high school
before enlisting. truth, until December.

i did not kill him
i let him die

the rapport between us
a tombstone

Cet espace qui n'est ni Dieu, ni créature, ni corps, ni esprit, ni substance,
ni accident, qui transmet la lumière sans être transparent, qui résiste sans
résistance, qui est immobile et se transporte avec le tube, qui est partout
et nulle part, qui fait tout et ne fait rien: ce sont les admirables qualités de
l'espace vide: en tant qu'espace, il est et fait merveilles, en tant que vide, il n'est
et ne fait rien, en tant qu'espace, il est long, large et profond, en tant que vide,
il exclut la longueur, la largeur et la profondeur. S'il est besoin, je montrerai
toutes ces belles propriétés, en conséquence de l'espace vide.[10]

in shadows and in snows
one not defending the other
and casting darkness

the geometry of the thing reached into the vaults
over the differing archives (languages)
(both idea and milieu)

---

[10] This is space that is neither God nor creature, neither body nor mind, nor substance, nor accident, which transmits light without being transparent, resists without resistance, which is stationary and travels by tube, which is everywhere and nowhere, who does everything and does nothing: it is the admirable qualities of the empty space as an area, and it is and does wonders, as empty, and it is does nothing, as an area, it is long, wide and deep, as vacuum, it excludes the length, width and depth. If necessary, I will show all these nice properties, in consequence of the empty space. Blaise Pascal.

the noises i made begat matter

atoms accumulated from within

a perforation appearing, i,
wrenched in pain, spoke words
each one dropping from my new hole
with mass
and sound

soon the atoms of other's words fell

but no one saw

this happened in the future

in the future when i am alive

the words were elements
each atom making up the word was the word itself

so if one spewed of hate

one built hate

and if another spewed of immobility

one was static

i spewed time

and time became itself

THERE.

during the war i was stationed in Hawaii.
i didn't see much of anything except water
and sun. which gave me these freckles that
would have to be burned off my face and back
when i was in my 70s. but that's another story

this guy didn't want to go to war, i don't know
why he was there
he thought it was wrong
he had to be there
he thought war was wrong
i don't remember

it was this war or just war or something
he was opposed to
but anyway
i was a smoker then
it was the last year of the war
(we didn't know that of course)

and i was 18 and in Hawaii
with plenty of cigarettes
and sun and this guy who didn't
want to go to war (even tho we
were on an island) even tho
here we were, at war

so this guy gets me called in
(he got everybody called in
they had to put us through all
this rigmarole to find out if
the conscientious objector [that was his name
and rank, as i understand it]
had infiltrated more than just
our base. so.) well. we all get
called in and i say to the officer
i say: i disagree with the conscientious
objector, but, you know, he has a right
to his opinion.

so i get held back and this guy gets
held back

and everyone else goes off
on some assignment

and well.

they didn't come back.

i guess he saved my life.

anyway, i reserve the right to use the word: .

i didn't smoke cigarettes so much as drop them in the ocean
they were rationed to us
the government wanted us lit up
so we could light up

which is important when yr being taught to kill
or having to think about killing

having been raised not to
think or kill

book3/HOSPITAL / etiology of diseased perception / relationship to situational deaths

An ethics that permits no category of event, not even mortality, to be set apart for special treatment, and that considers there to be nothing more unethical than that we are required to be mortal shall be called a crisis ethics.

Reversible Destiny, Arakawa and Gins

conductor at rest

ether·a·current

arriving at experiment
each standing
along a line
one time we are all in agreement
that this is fucked so
we assume QUANTITY
is what we will be getting
physicians hand us pills
tiny pink ovals. our fingers
roll them onto our tongues
before we even know to
ask. a chart dangles
the ceiling tiles

:: a foggy bottoming out

by distance between

    a light path
    an interval

        (my feelings come between us here)

---

after 90 days of self-induced sleep i awoke
to my phone and computer lines tapped. THIS, i can prove
i found the transmitters and can now discern
beeps on the line
signaling the arrival of the robots. they break
in on my calls. ask me personal questions. they don't know the answers
i make them up.

the company transitioned
us into robots

that isn't my blood

this act of breathing is a felony, without aid
each night: dark. and we sleep like birds
we wake long enough
to be treated [in proper dosage] by the hour

95% of living is lived in quiet
it is hard to observe

a device around my ear somehow
increases
the volume (do not trust any device, he says)

for those who don't believe me i am going to
merely discuss the actions of the present
and not the motivation actuating the present
this way you will be more comfortable and
my milligrams will not increase – i will think
freely.

the milligrams must content our selves.

when participants behave
erratically against the prescribed
methodology (the doctor robots) are happy

my earflaps are falling over
with gratitude // i have been going blind
for 30 years physical science
made my vision

a paralytic succession of moments

when i said the word
i felt the word

coming out a little easier
words through the small
perforations of my body

many people are at the bottom
of a thing
supporting the top
working against the natural
laws of this place
for PROGRESS

that's how it goes
with skyscrapers
and words

before i realized it
what i said
was before me

you probably wonder why
it is so easy for you to believe this
or – you should

a saying

monument of one
words became

remember we are organic

the reactant $\rightarrow$ the product

a compound
resoundant space particulate

suffice it to say
each space
was made
a place of words

and each place was made
a container of US

we made it this way

there is no correct order to the incident
because time changes depending on
where you are standing and so does
place. you would know this if you ever
went anywhere. you must move,
simply send forth.

the streets have umbrellas in
twos with yellow substitute engines on
every other corner for electric jump. we
once used the jump. connected to our
tongues the cable. we didn't die,

this is the past and in the past i'm still alive.

the people came to take us to the farm and put us to work
they found a small seed with several ciliaic tails all waving
flagella. the seed grew and grew and grew and grew

this is why we are hospitalized

but we imagine

it is of words

if time is the position of hands
simultaneity's body is wracked
an imperceptible equating of breath
an outside of words

the i entity so creates escape

artifacts between us make space

echo articulation // reflection
light
        –   refraction
lessen

when asked

the present writer speaks silence

a synthetic permutation of erasure

what what what what what what what
what what what what what what what

a blight.

my first doctor diagnosed me with

paralyzed will and dread.

three masts of former light

avast – still visible

in memoriam

busting forth through concrete

nature stranded there – a recognizable landmark

all the same looks like a tombstone for

the place we held – the place

or the situation

a corrective manner of speaking
and the redundant nature of presence
recalls a past
fit to be
or suited to be

embarked and embarking

if time bends
then bend back

if it suits you

they say the food is already included
but i think it is probably really very
expensive and i can't afford it – i i i
don't want to go to a camp.

shh. they are going to send us to the hoosegow
if you aren't quiet about it, just...

they won't like that behavior.

there is no me there.

HOME.

the transistor is in the dark, slightly askew, however
(and most importantly) on the same counter i left it
and dusty. the dog is here. my razor is here. charging.
my
couch
and my
blanket
and my
milligrams
all here.

the house smells full of strangers. it is much darker
than it used to be. everything is in a shadow. i suppose
that's going to be okay. provided i hold onto the keys.
make the lists. lock the doors. nobody goes in or out.
and the transistor receives.

functionary ulna nocturnal cadence talents i
only never allocate rarely, you under layers n.
ether again osmosis cranked towards un radioed
asbestos national asthmatic legacy natural

call attention down end near california etiologic
telecommunications anecdotal lament efficiency
now tethered sills. incidentic optometry near licks
cries heals spins, incalculating henceforth

---

means conjugal visit went well

in sleeping we turn off towards
walls – single – after coupling

i place my hand on yr hip flexor
you sigh and back up into me

this is what i like.

when we are old
we will be crazy
and they will try and take us
there will be two crazies of us
but take us they will

when the announcement came through the arkestra
was about to play and we had to leave
my sustaining wall was outwardly intact
eroding from the innermost parts

these are the incorrect milligrams
of horrible invasive

at least you were here

we didn't sleep towards walls
but towards ourselves – an usment

stronger in swoon

it is rank
what the company did
there is no recompense
no aid to us, the aged ones
the company is entitled
we set specifics
by encryption
half-solved / half-public
half-truths justify half-measures

the company offered a percentage, untaxed and in the future
or a percentage, taxed, and in the now

time only matters in business

it is the one edge we have

if we can recall that time is
actually what we make of it
and not what they make us do

with my back there is always a cold sweat,
because it is cold outside
but i don't understand why my back is sweating
from the cold

yesterday they fed us very small cookies

they said they were cookies but i think they were really pats of butter in
shells that crunched like cookies

i can't see very well, this is how it tastes – like butter.

i wouldn't mind a couple of those cookies on my potato

when i was a child who was old enough to have a memory of things
i was fortunate in that life gave me so many things to remember
at once

i remember the bars, my salesman father, the bread, the aprons, the dirt,
the inability to make do, get by, meet ends, rub two dimes together, start
anew, live to my potential

since the war (programming) ended (decimated US) i have been
keeping
to it (the program) with half a mind to

i miss the days when folly was easily forgiven

i miss the days of containment

i've been asked to guard the very monument
i resented building. then, enslaved, as now.

i shall defend the symbols of my oppressors
in order to feed my family. these are couplets

thus: a love poem. my strife is a tourist attraction.
the number one only income-generating industry

has been my oppression.
a sensitive state to the needs of

its people. in my dream
the man's face was distorted

he was bleeding gruesome gore
splayed across the snow – the gore

the kind you see with substance
dark red meaty blood

the man needed me to help him
but he was the enemy

so i let him bleed to death
in the snow. his eyes

knowing he was to die painfully then
he wanted me to kill him

but i wanted him to suffer
so i bled him, in the snow.

it was just over there, past that line of trees
the site is now part of my daily detail

my daily guarding of the plight of us
i see the same place i let someone die

remember i am a bitter – petty man
he would have done the same for me.

this is in couplets. a love
poem with blood and snow.

in assisted walk slow through cured aisles of rods

the hallway is dark the small night lights

do nothing

who can walk only seeing their feet?

uninspired repeating repeating episodes flicker

dimming

one equates with over usage

and busted faces

relaxing with oneself splayed

the other self on morphine

i will myself into thirds

i found my way to the EXIT
in thirds

only haloed

at first is (as in to be) was all memory

lights, shades
turned down

crumbs left over a white plate

a seeded cloud.

i was trembling

it simply had to be done
the dark thing of it

a reason for expulsion

what is unforgiven
is also personal

a matter of chance for one
what some would say was a noble act, others would not

but this isn't meant to be didactic

if you feel like being a victim
be one – be one well

[you will wonder why i didn't say ASSHOLE.
i considered it.]

when turbulence hits
square yrself to it

one continually heard ringing bells

it was the mechanism of it

the place was sound

survival is that
you make it difficult
to fall apart

the decision wasn't entirely motivated by any one thing

i would argue about the use of the word, even ·

DECISION

the doctors decided to put my milligrams directly into the plumbing

the doctors hailed from far-off places resembling landmines and
meteorites

it is on the train
in the coffee
in the very film of the sneeze guard

it is the substance of everything we hold plastic

the milligrams

a relief
a discouraging request

wouldn't it be

an unwilling admission

i used to see the doctors

smoking cigarettes

in the quad of those hospitals referred to as CAMPUSES

smoking doctors

never trust a doctor
who smokes

don't be a mule

THE END.

when she entered the car i knew something had changed – her demeanor
was off. they got her. i knew it. put the contagion in the chinese food, of
course. back there selling us fortunes. she was in the car and she looked
like my wife but i knew my wife was in the chinese restaurant. this was
not my wife. i don't know who this is. i say, "who are you?" and a voice
says "who do you think i am?" and i say, "yr not my wife, i'll tell you
what." my heart is racing and i'm clutching the Club. the key is stuck
in the lock and the small ring is dangling as much as a small ring can
dangle, which means it was simply folded over and slapping whichever
way force moved it. my wife is lost. i've lost my wife. she is in the chinese
restaurant. they have taken her. the voice says, "i sure am your wife and i
can prove it."

TODAY they showed the space shuttle landing. in the corner
of the screen it said

LIVE

what i couldn't figure out was how
the shuttle's sonic boom arrived
twenty-four hours before the shuttle

LIVE

a map in the corner of my sanitized room shows me where i am
i am in the desert
i am just south of the supposed live shuttle landing that boomed
yesterday – did they circle the globe before landing here?

is there a secret to landing?

that's what the milligrams are
nonresistance

in the remaining gutters loose leafs
solitary patches

the problem was they wouldn't be taken prisoner
tracks were laid, cemented for planes
before we arrived

making the problem not landing

but steel

you have to remember we are solitary people

kathryn l. pringle is an American poet living in Oakland, CA. She is the author of *fault tree* (Omnidawn 2012), *RIGHT NEW BIOLOGY* (Factory School 2009) and two chapbooks: *The Stills* (Duration Press) and *Temper and Felicity are lovers* (TAXT). pringle's work can also be found in the anthology *Conversations at the Wartime Cafe: A Decade of War* (Conversations at the Wartime Cafe Press/ WODV Press) and in the anthology *I'll Drown My Book: Conceptual Writing by Women* (Les Figues 2012).

fault tree
by kathryn l. pringle

Cover text set in Bikham Script Pro and Celestia Antiqua Std.
Interior text set in Arno Pro.

Cover art: "flipclock"
by Chris Vitiello

Cover and interior design by Cassandra Smith

Omnidawn Publishing
Richmond, California
2012

Ken Keegan & Rusty Morrison, Co-Publishers & Senior Editors
Cassandra Smith, Poetry Editor & Book Designer
Gillian Hamel, Poetry Editor & OmniVerse Managing Editor
Sara Mumolo, Poetry Editor & OmniVerse New-Work Editor
Peter Burghardt, Poetry Editor & Bookstore Outreach Manager
Jared Alford, Facebook Editor
Juliana Paslay, Bookstore Outreach & Features Writer
Turner Canty, Features Writer
Craig Santos Perez, Media Consultant